Banded Sea Snake

By Juliet Figorito

Gareth Stevens
Publishing

Please visit our website, www.garethstevens.com. For a free color catalog of all our high-quality books, call toll free 1-800-542-2595 or fax 1-877-542-2596.

Library of Congress Cataloging-in-Publication Data

Figorito, Juliet.
Banded sea snake / Juliet Figorito.
    p. cm. — (Killer snakes)
Includes index.
ISBN 978-1-4339-5623-2 (pbk.)
ISBN 978-1-4339-5624-9 (6-pack)
ISBN 978-1-4339-5621-8 (library binding)
1. Sea kraits—Juvenile literature. I. Title.
QL666.O64F55 2011
597.96′4—dc22

                             2010045996

First Edition

Published in 2012 by
Gareth Stevens Publishing
111 East 14th Street, Suite 349
New York, NY 10003

Copyright © 2012 Gareth Stevens Publishing

Designer: Michael J. Flynn
Editor: Greg Roza

Photo credits: Cover, p. 1 Mike Stevens/The Image Bank/Getty Images; (pp. 2–4, 6, 8, 10, 12, 14, 16, 18, 20–24 snake skin texture), pp. 18–19, 21 Shutterstock.com; p. 5 Norbert Wu/Science Faction Jewels/Getty Images; p. 7 Reinhard Dirscherl/Visuals Unlimited/Getty Images; p. 9 Travel Ink/Gallo Images/Getty Images; p. 11 James R. D. Scott/Flickr/Getty Images; p. 13 Photolibrary/Getty Images; p. 15 David B. Fleetham/Photolibrary/Getty Images; p. 17 iStockphoto.com.

Printed in the United States of America

CPSIA compliance information: Batch #CS11GS: For further information contact Gareth Stevens, New York, New York at 1-800-542-2595.

Contents

Snake of the Sea 4

Snake Colors 8

Life Underwater 10

Going Ashore. 12

On the Hunt 14

Heads or Tails? 18

People and Banded Sea Snakes. . 20

Glossary 22

For More Information 23

Index 24

Boldface words appear in the glossary.

Snake of the Sea

Did you know that some snakes live underwater? They're called sea snakes. There are more than 50 kinds of sea snakes in the world. The banded sea snake belongs to a group called sea kraits. It makes a deadly **venom** inside its body.

5

Banded sea snakes live in warm ocean waters. They're commonly found close to land in the eastern Indian Ocean and the southwestern Pacific Ocean. Adult snakes can grow to about 10 feet (3 m) long and weigh up to 11 pounds (5 kg).

Snake Colors

A banded sea snake is blue or blue gray with black bands, or stripes. The snake's belly is yellow or cream colored. The banded sea snake's head is black. Its upper lip and face are often yellow. In fact, it's sometimes called the yellow-lipped sea krait.

Life Underwater

The banded sea snake is made for life underwater. Its tail is flat like a paddle, which helps it swim. The banded sea snake's nose seals shut underwater. A large **lung** lets the snake stay underwater for at least 15 minutes at a time.

Going Ashore

Once every 10 to 14 days, banded sea snakes **slither** onto land. This makes them different from other sea snakes. They do this to let their food settle, **shed** their skin, or lay eggs. The banded sea snake is one of the few sea snakes that lays eggs on land.

13

On the Hunt

Banded sea snakes hunt just off the coast and near **coral reefs**. Their favorite food is eels, but they also eat crabs, small fish, and fish eggs. They swim along the sea floor, moving in and out of small cracks. When a banded sea snake finds a meal, it strikes!

15

The banded sea snake has very tiny **fangs**. However, it also has one of the strongest snake venoms in the world. One bite has enough venom to kill a big animal. Once the animal stops moving, the banded sea snake eats it whole.

17

Heads or Tails?

Several animals eat banded sea snakes, including large fish, sharks, and birds. The banded sea snake's head looks a lot like its tail. Animals sometimes go after the tail instead of the head. This allows the snake to escape—or turn and bite!

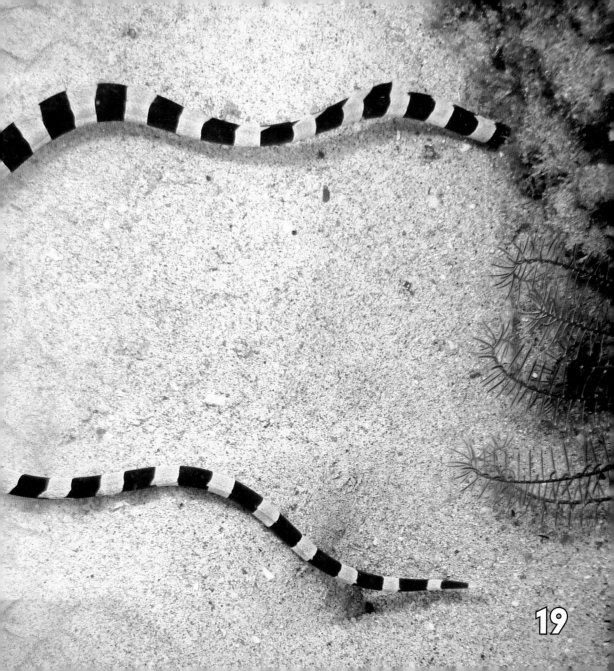

19

People and Banded Sea Snakes

Banded sea snakes don't often bite people, but they will if they feel they're in danger. Most bites happen to fishermen who find the snakes caught in their nets. One bite can be deadly unless the person takes a drug to fight the venom.

Snake Facts
Banded Sea Snake

Length	up to 10 feet (3 m) long
Weight	up to 11 pounds (5 kg)
Where It Lives	warm waters of the southwestern Pacific Ocean and the eastern Indian Ocean
Colors	blue or blue gray with black bands; yellow or cream-colored belly; upper lip and face are often yellow
Killer Fact	Banded sea snakes sometimes bite themselves when hunting for eels. However, they aren't harmed by their own venom.

21

Glossary

coral reef: an underwater hill made up of the hard parts of tiny sea animals

fang: a long, pointed tooth

lung: a part of an animal that takes in air when it breathes

shed: to get rid of something

slither: to slide easily over the ground

venom: something a snake makes in its body that can harm other animals

For More Information

Books

Rake, Jody Sullivan. *Sea Snakes.* Mankato, MN: Capstone Press, 2007.

Sexton, Colleen. *Sea Snakes.* Minneapolis, MN: Bellwether Media, 2010.

Websites

Sea Snakes

www.animalcorner.co.uk/venanimals/ven_snakesea.html
Read more about sea snakes, including the banded sea snake.

Swimming with Sea Snakes

zoltantakacs.com/zt/tv/index.php?&idx=1
Read about a scientist's trip to the South Pacific to study the banded sea snake. The site includes pictures of his experiences.

Index

bands 8, 21

bite 16, 18, 20, 21

colors 8, 21

coral reefs 14

eels 14, 21

eggs 12, 14

fangs 16

fishermen 20

food 12, 14

head 8, 18

hunt 14, 21

Indian Ocean 6, 21

land 12

lung 10

nose 10

Pacific Ocean 6, 21

people 20

sea kraits 4

shed 12

tail 10, 18

venom 4, 16, 21

yellow-lipped sea krait
    8